SISTER WENDY'S
MEDITATIONS
on the
MYSTERIES
of
OUR FAITH

Sister Wendy Beckett

Liguori

LIGUORI, MISSOURI

Imprimi Potest: Thomas D. Picton, C.Ss.R.
Provincial, Denver Province, The Redemptorists

Published by Liguori Publications, Liguori, Missouri
www.liguori.org

Library of Congress Cataloging-in-Publication Data

Beckett, Wendy.
    Sister Wendy's meditations on the mysteries of our faith / Wendy Beckett.—1st ed.
        p.   cm.
    ISBN-13: 978-0-7648-1577-5
    1. Lent—Meditations. 2. Lent—Art. 3. Easter—Meditations 4. Easter—Art. I. Title.
II. Title: Meditations on the mysteries of our faith.
    BV85.B385 2007
    242'.34—dc22   2006032987

Image credits: *Temptation on the Mountain* (p. 8), © The Frick Collection, NY; *Agony in the Garden* (p. 12), © Scala/Art Resource, NY; *Christ and the Woman of Samaria* (p. 16), © Museo-Thyssen-Bornemisza, Madrid; *Healing of the Blind Man* (p. 20), © National Gallery Picture Library, London; *The Raising of Lazarus* (p. 24) by Duccio di Buoninsegna, 1310-11, 17 ⅛ x 18 ¼ © 2006 Kimbell Art Museum, Fort Worth, TX; *The Entry Into Jerusalem* (p. 28), © Scala/Art Resource, NY; *Three Marys at the Tomb* (p. 32), © Scala/Art Resource, NY; *Noli Me Tangere* (p. 36), © Scala/Art Resource, NY; *Journey to Emmaus* (p. 40), © Scala/Art Resource, NY; *Apparition Behind Closed Doors* (p. 44), © Scala/Art Resource, NY; *Incredulity of Thomas* (p. 48), © Scala/Art Resource, NY; *Apparition to the Apostles at the Sea of Tiberias* (p. 52), © Scala/Art Resource, NY; *The Ascension* (p. 56), © Scala/Art Resource, NY; *The Coming of the Holy Spirit* (p. 60), © Scala/Art Resource, NY.

Printed in Mexico
11 10 09 08 07   5 4 3 2 1
First edition

CONTENTS

INTRODUCTION

D on't let the small size of this book fool you! It brings together two unlikely but significant "celebrities" born centuries and continents apart yet united in a love of the mysteries of our faith, their impact on humanity and, perhaps most importantly, the way these realities are communicated in the art of painting.

Sister Wendy Beckett was born in South Africa in 1930. Only relatively late in life did she decide to pursue her favorite subject of art. She gained her "celebrity status" through a series of acclaimed art history documentaries for the BBC in the nineties that were later shown around the world, including on the PBS network.

Duccio di Buoninsegna (c. 1255–1319) spent most of his life in the Tuscan city of Siena. At this time, Siena rivaled its neighbor to the north, Florence, for political and artistic dominance in Italy. From various city records it seems that Duccio may have played a significant role in both of these arenas. He is considerered by many today as the first of the great names in Italian painting.

Duccio's masterpiece, *The Maestà*—a large altarpiece painted for the cathedral in Siena—was completed in 1311. Sister Wendy uses fourteen episodes in the history of our salvation in Christ from the reverse side of this huge panel (sixteen feet by sixteen feet) as a basis for her meditations in this book.

The complementarity of text and image presented on these pages brings into focus the almost paradoxical juxtaposition of the mysteries of our faith: darkness and light, falsity and truth, dying and rising, humanity and divinity, Lent and Easter. These were all very vivid and concrete dimensions of daily life in the Middle Ages. Here, Sister Wendy offers them again to help us grasp—in ourselves, in one another, in our day and place—the reality and presence of God.

THE EDITOR

SISTER WENDY'S
MEDITATIONS
on the
MYSTERIES
of
OUR FAITH

TEMPTATION ON THE MOUNTAIN
(or in the Desert)

Lent begins with Ash Wednesday, serving as a prelude to the First Sunday of Lent. It ends forty days later with the Triduum of Holy Thursday, Good Friday, and Holy Saturday as a separate and solemn climax. We live in Lent for forty days in memory of the forty days Jesus spent in the desert, when he set himself to work out what was his Father's will for him, and to encounter, unprotected, the full force of temptation. (He chose forty days, of course, in honor of that sacred forty years in which the Israelites wandered in the desert, seeking the Promised Land.)

Matthew's Gospel is quite explicit: he was led by the Spirit into the desert "to be tempted," and the temptations are grouped for us into three: to turn stones into bread, to throw himself from the Temple, trusting that the angels would "bear him up," and to choose between taking possession of the world in security, but with obeisance to Satan, or risking everything on his own efforts.

Duccio here shows us this last and greatest trial. Jesus has been lifted aloft, onto a "high mountain," the very sort of magical trick that he resolutely refused in the other temptations. Here he has been given no choice: the devil has seized him and carried him. The sheer loathsomeness of this evil figure shows what this contact, this being forced to endure, must have cost our Lord. His face is very somber, and he clutches his cloak to his body as if to defend himself against contamination. We ourselves can so easily feel soiled by the thoughts that come to us unbidden and unwanted, and we think God is displeased with us. But no: here is the holy Son of God suffering just these intrusions of thought into his privacy, and all he can do is what we can do: reject them.

Darkness and Light

These vile thoughts are given visual form by the artist: in a world of lovely light, Satan is a moving darkness, an emptiness on the landscape. The landscape is one of Duccio's most enchanting inventions. He knows his Italy, his own Siena, and the small hill towns that fill the Tuscan countryside. They represent that world the devil offers Jesus, enclaves of human life, beautiful when seen from without, but inside, hotbeds of envy, anger, pride. Duccio, himself a turbulent man, often in trouble with the authorities, knew all about the sad reality of his beautiful Italy.

Jesus must have longed with all his heart to establish in the world the kingdom of his Father, where there would be only love, justice, truth, to maintain the restless heart of man *in peace*. He must have realized, from watching John the Baptist, how slow and unsatisfactory would be the progress. The sadness in his face comes from knowing what it will cost to bring the world to the Father, and how much of this beloved world would never come. The temptation is to let the end justify the means. A token bow to evil and *such good would result*. This is a genuine temptation, one that our Lord would never yield to, but which so many of us do. We see it in history; we see it in our lives. But when Jesus raises his hand in repudiation, it is for us that he makes the refusal, as an example and as a support. When we are tempted, his gesture strengthens us, holding us back from that first dangerous step that leads to sin. "He was tempted in every way that we are," says holy Scripture, "but without sin." In the desert, hungry and alone, Jesus concentrated on his goals; he examined his life and possible future. We are taken into Lent each year to urge us to do the same.

THE AGONY
IN THE GARDEN

When Jesus is tempted in the desert, we see him rejecting the devil with majestic serenity; he is fully in command of himself: weakening is not on any possible agenda. We, too, understand that sin must be rejected, but how differently we often react. For us, there is usually no intense self-command, and so we feel, even if we do resist, that we are blameworthy.

Of all the events in the life of Jesus, the Agony in the Garden is the most comforting. We are often told how the martyrs suffered joyfully, how the saints desired to suffer. There is nothing of this in the garden. Duccio shows Jesus twice. On the left, he is confronting the reality of his isolation. His three closest friends are sleeping, leaving him more alone than if he were by himself. He comes to them for support: they are indifferent. On the right, we see the terrible struggle in which he is hoping to be strengthened. Duccio shows Jesus kneeling on hard rock, with the orange trees of the garden out of touch. His face is gaunt with anguish. He no longer holds out an imperious arm, bidding Satan to depart, he holds up two pleading hands, begging his Father to spare him the terrible death that is all but inescapable.

Some artists depict the angelic comfort that is offered at the end, when Jesus has stammered out, through tears and sweat, an expression of his deepest heart's desire, to do the will of his Father. Duccio makes that comfort very small and remote. The little angel is hardly there; our Lord must find his support within himself. This emotional turmoil is very unlike the admired attitudes of the saints that we are called upon to admire.

Jesus does not *want* to suffer, and although he consents as soon as he is certain that this is how his life is meant to end—in pain and disgrace, humanly speaking—he does not pretend that it is easy. His brow is furrowed, his body tense. There is a slight touch of scarlet on his neck and throat, which is Duccio's subtle reminder to us that the gospels say: "His sweat ran down as if it were blood."

Endurance

A Lord who suffered with joy would be of little help to us who shrink from pain. Pain in itself is never pleasing to, or willed by, God. It happens, this pattern of the world as it is, and in that pain God is with us, enduring it and supporting us. We, too, have an (almost) unseen angel, because we have the example of Jesus, showing us that everything can be endured, if we keep our gaze fixed on God.

As we enter more deeply into Lent, the need to think out what we are doing with our lives and what drives us can become overlaid. But it remains crucial. Life is short, and how we use it is up to us. There are no friends or relatives to take responsibility away, to bear the blame for our failure, to be relied on for infallible guidance. Facing the truth and accepting its demands may be extremely difficult and even painful. Duccio leaves us in no doubt that Jesus, the Son of God, was racked with sorrow and fear. But he clung to the love of his Father, who is our Father too. The praying hands of Jesus are also offering hands, surrendering hands, and he will achieve the same in us, if we let him.

CHRIST AND THE
WOMAN OF SAMARIA

This is an image we all understand. Jesus is tired and thirsty, too tired to go on with the apostles into the town to get food. He sits at Jacob's well, and asks the Samaritan woman for a drink. As the story continues, he reads her soul and tells her that he will give her "living water," which she does not understand.

Duccio shows the apostles coming out of the city with their bundles of food, looking as uncomprehending as the woman. Why is Jesus talking to *her*, they wonder, and what does he mean? The exchange of glances between Jesus and this stranger makes it clear to us why he is speaking to her. She is, apparently, exactly the kind of woman that the apostles would not waste their time on. She is an "unbeliever," in that the Jews thought the Samaritans were heretics. She is, moreover—and Jesus knows but they do not—of low repute locally (when she first tries to tell her fellow townsfolk about Jesus, they will not listen to her) and the kind of argumentative female that insists on answering back. But she is one of the lost sheep that he was sent to gather to himself, and he ignores his fatigue to explain to her what the Scriptures really mean.

The living water, of course, is grace, that interior

gift that God gives us freely and unasked. It is ours for the taking. Our Lord has worn himself out, and will soon die on the cross, solely so that we might "drink of this water and never die." Physically we shall all die, hard thought it is to believe. But spiritually, Jesus has redeemed us from death and made heaven sure for us.

If we feel that we are not the kind of person that is worthy of our Lord's attention, then this is a picture to enlighten us. Jesus takes a passionate interest, is indeed profoundly in love, with each of us. The tragedy is that this is a love we abuse. The woman here is not particularly receptive. We know that she claims Jesus convinces her, but who can tell how fully she allowed those living waters to flow as the years went by and she did not see him again?

Images of Prayer

Saint Teresa of Ávila saw the well and its waters, Jesus and his interior waters, our thirst and his desire to give, as *images of prayer*. Yet grace cannot fill those dry reaches of our spirit unless we ask for it. The asking is precisely what we mean by prayer. It can be spoken, asking: "Lord, give me this water…" as the woman prays, or it can be *an unspoken need, a looking at* God that expresses silently all our longing. Longing need not be emotionally experienced. It is sometimes an act of the will, accepting that *we are far from what* God wants us to be, even from what we want ourselves to be, and acknowledging that the grace of God can transform us. But we must take time to let the grace shine on us, the water to seep deep within. Lent is the season when we look at our prayer habits. Is there any space in our day to be silent and let God give his grace? Even ten minutes, holding ourselves still before him, or a final act of repentance, gratitude, and love before the day ends, are expressions of a need that he longs only to satisfy.

HEALING OF THE BLIND MAN

Many of us see blindness as the most incapacitating of afflictions, and the gospels show Jesus as quick to offer relief. He often healed at a distance, with a word, but for the blind beggar it is a hands-on healing. We are told that he moistened his finger with saliva, his own body substance, and anointed the useless eyes.

Duccio sees the entire band of apostles huddled together in an awestruck clump, while Jesus crosses the space between the blind man and himself and gently rubs his finger over his eyes. The man—who cannot see what is happening but can surely hear the strange hush and also feel the damp touch—lifts his hand in amazement. Then Duccio gives us the sequel, when the man drops the stick on which he had been totally dependent all these years, and looks up in bewilderment at the visual world. He does not turn to Jesus; he is too overwhelmed by the brightness of the light and the shapes of the city. This is a man reborn: he has much with which to come to terms.

Although there are the apostles and several buildings in the background, this is essentially only a picture of Jesus and the blind man, the man's need, his patience, his surrender to the touch of this stranger, and the concentration of our Lord. We can see that he wants very much to restore his sight, and that it is not done without an effort. He is giving himself as completely as the beggar can receive him.

Seeing the Truth

Making the blind man see was one of the signs Jesus quoted to the friends of John the Baptist when they came asking to know who he was. For him, as for all of us, it is a symbol. We readily call "blind" someone who shuts his eyes to the truth. But which of us can dare claim that we "see the truth"? You must be part of it or you would not be reading this book! But the whole truth? The truth with a capital letter that Jesus identified with himself: "I am the Way, the Truth, and the Life." The truth is immensely vast and challenging. Would we be eager to see our conduct, our fulfillment of our responsibilities, our unselfishness, as God sees these things? If there is no glaring wrongness, do we not quite happily jog along, conscience clear?

The great thing about the blind beggar was that he knew he was blind; he cried out, however hopelessly in human terms, to be given sight. Jesus spoke sadly of those who have eyes yet do not see. This is us. He accepts this, he understands it, he feels compassion for it. But he cannot heal it unless we actually acknowledge it and ask for light. Lent has always been regarded as a time for confession, for what is now called the sacrament of penance and reconciliation. One reason for this is that we cannot go to confession unless we look into our hearts and see where we are falling short. Recognizing our failures is the first step to allowing the grace of God to purify us.

We all have a stick and a begging purse. If we allow our Lord to cure our blindness, we can throw both away. Notice how bent the man was before the miracle, and how straight he stands afterward. True sorrow, true amendment, absolution, a new, seeing life: there is nothing our Lord wants more than to work this miracle in you.

THE RAISING
OF LAZARUS

Opening a new grave is not something we like to think about. The very smell is repulsive, and Duccio does not shrink from showing the nearest spectator gagging at the smell. Even the sisters of the corpse, Martha and Mary, dear friends of Jesus, who have begged him to help their brother Lazarus, seem anxious to hold him back. It is too late, they remonstrate, your friend is dead: why did you not come when we asked you, Lord, when there was still time?

John's Gospel tells us that Jesus wept when he heard that Lazarus was dying, but he stayed away, silent, until it was "too late." This is the most dramatic miracle in the whole story of Jesus, and Duccio gives it its full tension. There is a crowd, nervously expectant; there are the almost hostile sisters and a dubious Peter; and there is Jesus, commanding the grave to be opened and summoning forth the dead man. Daringly, Duccio depicts Lazarus as not yet fully restored, neither alive nor dead, a dead man who can stand, swathed in his mummy cloths, but whose eyes stare wildly, without recognition. It is a tragic face, and we long to be there in the next few minutes, when life and animation—joy perhaps?—will come back to it.

Two Risings

Only the Gospel of John reports this extraordinary event, setting it very close to the time when Jesus himself was laid in a tomb, from which he, too, would rise. But the two risings are very different. Lazarus is resuscitated. He was dead, he has been given life again, and that life will come to an end. Lazarus will die sometime in the future. But Jesus is resurrected. He rises to a new life, an absolute life that is infinite, the life of heaven that we (and Lazarus too) will know one day, but not now. What Jesus is revealing here is his power. To save his friend from dying of his sickness would have been miracle enough, we would think, but Jesus needed to go further. The time was fast coming when his apostles and friends would not see him in bodily form, when they would have to understand what it means to call him "My Lord and my God." This incomprehensible act of divine power was for their sake, to help them believe after the crucifixion in the long years ahead.

It can also have, for us, a personal meaning. If Lent is the time for looking into our lives and chasing what is wrong, then the great danger is despair.

All too quickly can we think that there is nothing much we can do: "I'm like that." We may want to be better, but feel a change of life is simply beyond us. Remember Lazarus was dead, decaying, buried. Yet Jesus could call him forth into a newness of life at will. Never think that our own will can make significant changes. Habits and weaknesses bind us fast. (Like Lazarus in his tight swathings.) But the whole point of being a Christian, and Lent repeats this again and again, is that it is not on our own will that we rely. It is God who wills goodness for us, God who will achieve it. All we have to do is ask and, like dead Lazarus, stand up in our mortal coffin and let God make everything different.

THE ENTRY
INTO JERUSALEM

In the *Maestà*, the great series of paintings of the life of our Lord and our Lady, that Duccio did for Siena Cathedral, there are only two that are double height. One is of the crucifixion, and the other is this one, the entry into Jerusalem. We repeat it in symbol in the liturgy, carrying palms, going in procession, singing hymns. It is the beginning of the most important week in human history, when Jesus died and rose again, when we were offered eternal safety and protection in the spirit of the risen Jesus. From now on, unless we reject his grace, we can be hurt but never truly damaged.

But I think there is another, lesser significance to which Duccio responds. This was the only time in the life of Jesus when he was wanted, welcomed, hailed. There are small boys busily tearing down branches for the people to wave, there is a man laying down his cloak for Jesus to ride over, and others preparing to do the same. There are the city elders, at the gates, hands raised in awed greeting. At the bottom of the painting, where we cannot help but see it, is a door conspicuously open. Jesus comes to his own city, which up to now has refused him, and they hail him triumphantly. He has grieved over Jerusalem, saying, with a smile, surely, that he was like a hen who wanted to shelter her chickens under her wings, and they "would not." But this day it would seem that they "would," and Jesus, for the only time in the gospels, rides a donkey, to receive their welcome.

Duccio shows his face as solemn, almost fraught. Did Jesus realize that it was only show? That within a few days these cries would ask for his death? The apostles raise their hands in wondering gratitude, but Jesus does no more than ride wearily on, a hand raised in blessing. (The happiest expression is on the face of the little donkey, which seems to be smiling to itself, as if the artist sees this bodily contact between animal and Jesus as the only reality of the story. Jesus is really and truly sitting on that rough and hairy back, and his presence cannot but be a blessing.)

A Crucial Decision

Palm Sunday of the Lord's Passion summons us to align ourselves either with Jesus or against him. It would seem that even to say "against" is ridiculous; are we not his followers? Well, perhaps we are not, really. Perhaps we are among the Jerusalemites who welcomed him when he seemed the Messiah who would magically take away their problems, but rejected him when he turned out to be a savior who carried a cross and died upon it, and asked those who loved him to do the same. Cheers and acclamations can pass as belief, but it is actions that count.

Lent asks us to scrutinize, calmly and in the presence of God, what direction our actions have led us and will lead us. Are we directed toward God? Or toward ourselves? Do we forgive? Do we pray? Do we try to be patient? The list is endless. Jesus offers his blessing to anybody who is sincere and seeks him. But what blessing can he give—however much he wants to—if we are only going through the motions, like the "good people" in Duccio's painting? Better to be an ass than a nominal Catholic!

THREE MARYS
AT THE TOMB

If you read histories of art and frequent museums, you will find countless paintings of the nativity and crucifixion but very few of the resurrection. You can understand why. Not only has nobody ever seen a resurrection, but the gospels only offer as their first evidence what they deduce from an empty tomb and folded grave clothes. What would a hypothetical eyewitness have seen? We have not the faintest idea.

This is not a real problem for writers, but it is an insurmountable one for painters. Some of the greatest have made an attempt, and their efforts look very inadequate. Duccio had no intention of looking inadequate. So his picture of the resurrection is the only one in the series in which the Lord himself is missing. "He is risen. He is not here."

It is, I think, the most beautiful of all Duccio's smaller works, and it cannily shows just the empty tomb, the angel and the three mourning women, all called Mary, who have come at break of day to anoint him. Behind the tomb rises sheer rock, and behind that the bright flame that speaks of what cannot be depicted. The angel points away: this is no time to be thinking of tombs. How it happened is unimportant; that it happened, all-important.

The women are not suffused with the joy we might expect either. It is too much, it is wonder of an order inconceivable. If Jesus really has risen, then the terrible weight of death that lies across every life has been lifted. It is not that he has died and come back to life again, like Lazarus. No, he has died and gone through death to eternity, and it is that alive-forever Jesus who will be the basis of all our own hope in an afterlife. It is as if the world's kaleidoscope had been given a final great twirl, and the whole pattern of being human is now changed. Now everything we do has meaning—it is done in the presence of a God who has proved he loves us— and yet nothing has meaning, apart from him.

The Challenge of Grace

We are offered joy too great to handle with ease, and we can see this on the three faces. Even the angel is awed, but the women are far more fearful than joyful. They clutch to themselves their small certainties, the jars of aromatic oil, their cloaks, the nearness of their friends. Perhaps it was far less disturbing to live with the grief of Jesus dead than to accept the rapture of Jesus alive. Any grace has a consequence: it is always for sharing, for reverent using. It is never just for ourselves. What would it mean to receive this particular grace, to be one of the three in the world who knew that Jesus had been raised? It is not so easy even to be one of the few Christians in our neighborhood who know.

What does God ask of us? The very least is that we should show in how we live that we have our eyes fixed on the Lord, and not only our own concerns. Others who are not so fortunate as we are should sense something in us that speaks to them of God.

The three Marys who came to anoint the body of Jesus saw an empty tomb. They also saw an angel, but for Mary Magdalene that was very poor recompense. She convinced herself that the body had been stolen and roamed the burial garden, crying and searching. Her eyes must have been swollen with tears, because when Jesus appeared to her she "mistook him for the gardener" and begged to know where Jesus was.

This is one of the most beautiful incidents in Scripture: Jesus in the first light of a spring day, coming up to his weeping disciple and calling her by her name. That word is enough. Mary drops to her knees and stretches out her longing arms, all her heart is set on embracing him. Jesus says to her: "Do not touch me—do not hold on to me—I am the dead-and-risen Jesus, and everything is different." In Latin: *Noli me tangere*.

Mary knows what those few words mean. As she looks more closely, she can see that her Jesus is the same but different. This is indeed the dead-and-risen Jesus, a Lord she must embrace only in her heart.

New Life

As Mary looks, she can see that his very garments gleam with inner brightness. Duccio is determined that we shall realize that our Lord is changed, that this is a spiritual body become visible. Already the harsh rocks are beginning to sprout with new life, plants and grasses, while on either side, almost like a guard of honor, two tall tress rear up. Jesus may seem to speak to Mary tersely, but his face is deeply compassionate. He is well aware what emotions rack her. The foremost is yearning. She does not kneel on both knees, but on one, tense with eagerness to spring to her feet and hold him in her arms. Her hands plead. But Jesus, standing so lightly on the ground, cannot be held. He has transcended the limitations he shared with us on earth, and it is in our hearts that we must encounter him.

Mary's posture, Mary's gesture, are perfect expressions of prayer. Prayer is a real communion with our Lord, but it is not a material one. We do not see him or touch him. But just as he looks at Mary with love, so does he look at us. She will not get what she wants, physical closeness, but what she does get is what she would want if she knew more.

She from now on will enter on a life of holiness that will make Mary Magdalene one of the Church's best-loved saints. A saint is only a man or woman who lives a life that is wholly God-directed. Whatever her previous distractions may have been, that is hereafter Mary's choice. Duccio shows her choosing Jesus, offering herself to him. She dimly realizes that it will mean carrying a cross, as in symbolic form he does here, and allowing the light of grace to change all her values, and she reaches out to the fulfillment of her destiny. Jesus transformed Mary, because she prayed; will he not transform us?

JOURNEY TO EMMAUS

We know the story of the journey to Emmaus: how two disciples, deeply distressed and despondent—all their hopes come to nothing—left Jerusalem and went home. (If not home, then anywhere out of this terrible city that killed the prophets.) They were joined on the way by a fellow traveler, who asked them what they were talking about. He drew them out, and they spilled the whole tragedy to him, ending with the account of what "the women" had seen—nothing—and their tales of angelic reassurance. They may have seen an angel, they conclude glumly, but they did not see Jesus.

Their fellow traveler replies at length, and many have been those who have longed to have heard the Scripture lesson that Jesus then gave, explaining how the Old Testament prefigured all that happened. They were still unaware who he was. Could it be that it was too dark? Or was it rather a closed mind? But even as a learned stranger, Jesus fascinates, and so they beg him, when he begins to say goodbye, to stay with him. They sit down at table, Jesus blesses the bread and breaks it—and they know. There is a moment of incredulous understanding, and then Jesus has disappeared, and the two forget all their fatigue and rush straight back to the city to tell Peter and the other apostles.

Was it really so sudden? And only when he broke the bread? They admit to themselves that their hearts were burning within them as they journeyed together and the stranger spoke to them about the Scriptures. This interior glowing must often have been a response to listening to Jesus speak. Perhaps they knew and did not know.

Enlightenment

Duccio has chosen an unusual episode in the narrative. Most artists show the table and the "Mass gesture" that opened their eyes, but Duccio clearly thinks enlightenment began earlier. They are still on the road, but they have come to an inn. Jesus, who is wearing the rough animal skins and scallop shell purse of a pilgrim, is making his farewell gesture, and it is up to them whether they stay with what he has already given them—so much enlightenment—or press for more. The two are almost nervously respectful. The older man, especially, looks most questioningly at Jesus: he suspects; at some level, he knows? The younger man points gravely to the open door of what will be an invaluable future.

If Jesus enters into that interior with them, there will be no further possibility of concealment. They will see, and they will have to face the challenge that vision always brings.

The stranger, an angel in disguise, is a legend in many cultures. But Jesus in disguise is a commonplace in Christianity. "Whatever you do to the least of my brethren, you do to me." The poor, unfed, the ill, neglected, the grieving, left without comfort—Jesus tells us that each time it is he who is so treated. Maybe every day he says something to us, directly or in what we see on TV or read. Yet we do not hear, because we are not listening for him. We are never told who the travelers to Emmaus were, but it is worth looking to their example and asking for a heart ready to respond to the Lord, in whatever form he chooses to come. We pray to see him, not to pass him by.

APPARITION BEHIND CLOSED DOORS

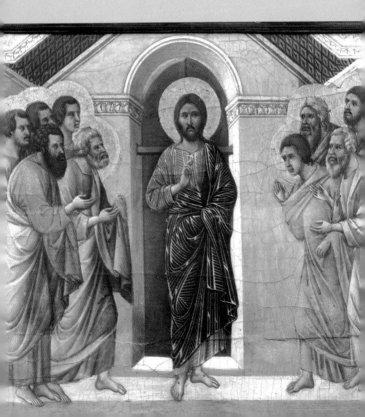

This is a very rare subject in art. Many painters have been attracted to the drama of Jesus appearing to Thomas to challenge his unbelief, but hardly any to the previous apparition when Jesus comes to his own in the upper room, Thomas being absent, and they have the first living proof that what the women have been saying—that unbelievable story—is actually true. John's Gospel emphasizes that the apostles were still very frightened. Enemies had killed Jesus, and they could well decide to do away with his followers also. They seem to be hiding out in the upper room, and they have the doors securely locked. The first indication that Jesus has not only risen but that this is a transcended Jesus comes from his heavenly ability to pass through closed doors.

Duccio obviously found the dynamics of this encounter fascinating. The locked doors are barred behind our Lord, and he stands framed by them. But his friends scatter to either side of the room aghast. No wonder that his first words are: "Peace be with you," and that a little later he has to repeat it. Saint John tells us that they were "overjoyed," but it is clearly a joy so "over," so enormous, that as yet their emotions are too limited to feel it. Frankly, they withdraw, trembling, the whites of their eyes very visible. Hands are raised in wonder, fear, reverence. They are speechless; they do not know where to put themselves. Soon Jesus will call notice to his wounds, the holy stigmata that make it inescapable that this is the very body that suffered on the cross. But Duccio is concerned with the first breathless moment when Jesus appears.

Living in the Present

It is all so familiar to us: we know what will come next and when the appearances will end (Ascension Thursday). We know how Peter, the gray-haired man on the left, with curls and a short beard, will grow in stature and become Saint Peter, the first pope. We know that young John, on the right, will write the most sublime of all the gospels and be the only apostle not to die a martyr's death. But they who were there could only live in the present, and what they were asked to do in that present was to look at Jesus and accept him.

Essentially, this is what God asks of us too. Our encounter may not be terrifying: easier perhaps if it were! God may offer the reality of his presence to us slowly, throughout a lifetime. We have been taught the doctrines of our faith, we have been helped to receive the sacraments, we have been in the congregation Sunday after Sunday for the homily. If we are sensible, we have read more about the faith now that we are adults: childhood instruction is all too often misremembered, or even inadequate. We should, unless we have been lazy, have a solid structure of intellectual belief. But is this all? Does what we believe affect our daily lives? Is it what guides our decisions? Can those who know tell from how we act that we are followers of Jesus? We can call ourselves Catholic and even come to Mass, and yet our lives may be motivated by exactly the same principles as people whose only driving force is ambition and selfishness. Duccio shows us men being changed, men accepting to be changed. It is the same Jesus who says "Peace" to us, if we would only listen, who says peace and gives peace. He stands in the upper room of our hearts, even if our doors are locked, and asks us to respond.

INCREDULITY
OF THOMAS

The story of the doubting Thomas spells out in capital letters the genuine leap of faith it took to believe in the resurrection. Jesus made that amazing first appearance in the upper room when Thomas was not present, and to the awe and excited reports of his friends, he raised a scoffing eyebrow. He clearly feels that they are too gullible. (I sometimes wonder if Thomas was a townsman rather than a simple fisherman like most of the apostles.) Thomas would have known how to assess the "evidence": "Unless I put my finger into the mark of the nails and into the wound in his side, I will not believe." Easy to say, when Jesus is not there. But to Thomas' consternation, Jesus not only reappears in the upper room, but he will not allow Thomas to wilt in the background. He summons him and repeats the challenge that Thomas had thought so private. Sheer embarrassment makes him touch and handle.

Duccio shows a nervous and shame-faced Thomas applying the most gingerly of fingers to our Lord's wounds, while Jesus regards him with sardonic gravity. It speaks well for the others that they are not smirking with "I told you so" expressions. (This encounter is too serious for anything petty.) It ends with an absolute declaration of faith: "My Lord and my God," and from Jesus, a kindly warning. Thomas is forgiven, that goes without saying: Jesus is an instinctive forgiver. But his doubt has meant that Thomas has missed the glory. It is those who have not seen who receive the blessing, and we are among those privileged believers.

Repentance

There is a lesson here about repentance. God will always forgive, and his love remains unaltered no matter what we do. But in doing what is against his will, we hurt ourselves. Our capacity for love is diminished. We can restore it, and that is the purpose of penance. It is not to set ourselves right with God, but to repair the spiritual hurt we have done to ourselves and perhaps to other people. (Think of a disobedient child climbing a tree and breaking a leg in a fall. However the parents make light of the disobedience, and the child is truly sorry, the leg stays in plaster.)

Some will say: what has Thomas done wrong? Doubt is often an excellent thing. Credulity is in-fantile: we all have to weigh evidence and make up our minds, and until we do, there is honest doubt, surely. But honest doubt is not willful doubt. Willful doubt is wrong precisely because it is not honest. It has an agenda, it is evading the truth for its own reasons. Jesus is quite stern with Thomas. He knows that the apostles struggled and then set their will on faith. Thomas obviously felt that he was better than Peter and the others, and his self-conceit tempted him into his foolish dare. Was there some reason why Thomas felt less threatened when he knew that Jesus was dead? Did the prospect of being an apostle, with all it entailed, secretly frighten him? If we are like him in his weakness, let us hope also to be like him in his strength, since Thomas died in the end for his faith.

APPARITION TO THE APOSTLES AT THE SEA OF TIBERIAS

Every apparition of Jesus during the forty days before the Ascension had a specific purpose. Perhaps we might have expected that one would take place by the seashore. We know for certain that at least a third of the apostles were fishermen and, apart from Matthew the tax collector, nearly all of them may have been. When Jesus wants a metaphor for their vocation as his followers, he says he will make them "fishers of men" and they seem to understand the relevance. In the Gospel of Luke, Peter's first summoning comes in the context of a miraculous draught of fish, and there are other miracles worked on the waters that the apostles know so intimately. In the days of waiting to see what postresurrection life will mean for them, ever-impatient Peter turns to fishing and his friends to go with him. They fish all night and catch nothing. As the sun rises a man on the shore, seen dimly through the morning mists, tells them where to throw the net. While they are struggling to deal with so enormous a haul, John, with the quick eyes of youth, tells Peter: "It is the Lord."

Duccio paints that pivotal moment: some straining with the net, some looking across with holy fear, John holding hand to heart in reverence, and Peter lashing resolutely through the water, arms raised in timid welcome. Jesus is hardly there. Duccio depicts him on the very edge of the painting. He gleams with the inward light of Godhead and beckons. For all the freshness and beauty of its setting (Jesus has a cooked picnic breakfast for them), this is a solemn encounter.

Humility

Jesus wants to give Peter the chance to erase the memory of his threefold denial during the trial that led to his death. When Peter denied Jesus, he suddenly remembered that Jesus had told him this would happen. Peter, buoyed up by emotional love, had stoutly affirmed total fidelity. Now he is wiser; he knows his weakness. We are told that he "wept bitterly" over his failure to support his Lord, and Jesus wanted that bitterness transformed into humility. Remorse is a corrosive emotion, repentance one that heals. So Peter is asked three times whether he loves his Lord, and three times, with growing distress, he affirms his faith. Each time, Jesus gives him a commandment, repeating with emphasis that it is Peter, despite all his flaws and—who knows?—even because of them, is to be the pastor of Jesus' flock. The image has changed from "fishing for men," one taken from a life they understand, to shepherding, a life that none of them seems to have experienced. Jesus adds a prophecy about martyrdom so that Peter knows exactly what he is being offered: not glory, not lordship, but a slow and painful death.

This is Jesus' last great attempt to teach his Church to be a servant Church, to see power as a grievous responsibility, a crushing burden that the chosen shepherd is called to bear for the sake of the kingdom. Jesus had told the Twelve that "I am among you as one who serves," but the desire for power is deep in human nature and the imperative to purify it deep in the Christian calling. This call to humility is not only for the pope, the bishops, the priests, and the theologians. Each of us has some power, even if only over our lives or perhaps just our own thoughts. Each of us is called by Jesus to let him burn away the pride within and let him draw from us the profound declaration of love that this morning conversation by the lake drew from Peter.

THE ASCENSION

The accounts of the Ascension, in three of the gospels (not John's) and the Acts of the Apostles, differ slightly, but the gist is very clear: Jesus gave them a final blessing and a commission, and then rose into the air, "until a cloud hid him from their sight." It is not an easy scene to make visible. The medieval painters managed by showing the apostles looking upward and two feet at the very top edge of the picture representing Jesus passing from earth to heaven. Unfortunately, the feet are not very impressive, aesthetically, and one can see that this image did not appeal to Duccio. What he gives us is rather indeterminate. It shows Jesus before he makes any movement upward. He is speaking with that unearthly authority that so riveted all who heard him. It *is* their word that will convert *the* waiting nations. It is they, up to now only followers, listeners to Jesus, who are now to take the pulpit and teach others, baptize others, do for them what Jesus has done in their own lives.

Duccio has Peter and another apostle (Matthew the evangelist?) holding a book. This small and reluctant group, bunched together for support, is already accepting the need to write down what *they* have witnessed and to accept this terrifying vocation with the utmost devotion to duty. They are standing very straight, their eyes fixed on Jesus for the last time in this life, and he seems half on tiptoe, ready for that dissolving of material ties in the glory of his Father.

Coming Home

Jesus had longed for this day. When he spoke to the apostles at the Last Supper, he spoke of them being in the world, and how he would send them his spirit, the Paraclete, to do within them what they could not do alone. To believe in the coming of the Spirit is one of his most emphatic messages. Yet, an undercurrent to the recognition that they are "in the world," is the quiet statement, made in prayer to the Father, "I am coming to you." Coming to the Father has been the great driving force of Jesus' life. That is where he is at home, that is where he belongs. He left the Father and all that heaven means so as to draw us out of our darkness and into his light, but how hard it must have been!

Right to the end, his chosen were squabbling about who "should be first." One was a traitor, his "Rock" had denied him, and all but John had run away. They were a feeble little band, but there was no more Jesus could do. He leaves them because they have all they need, and the Spirit will bring it to mind. But they themselves must do it. How God must long to do it for us, and make sure it is done! But that is never his way. We are independent moral beings, and if we use the abundance of grace that flows down upon us, we can become what Jesus is: a true child of God, someone who can echo these words: I am coming to you.

THE COMING OF
THE HOLY SPIRIT

As Jesus rose into life, he rose still higher, into heaven, making possible his last manifestation to us at Pentecost. It was a promised gift, the reality of his Spirit to teach us and inspire us, to be for us what Jesus had been for those who lived with him on earth. Jesus is just as truly present, but we cannot see or hear him. Our communication now is in prayer. In this last of the series, Duccio sees our Lady wearing the light-filled garment that distinguished the risen Jesus. None was ever closer to him than his mother, so close and so pure, beyond any other creature. She is aware of him in a way we can only imagine. No wonder the apostles cluster around her, enclosing her in their circle, able to receive the mighty force of the Spirit within her presence. The "mighty wind" that filled the whole house does not seem to disturb this waiting assembly. All seem wholly at peace, though several have a watchful eye on our Lady, trusting in her to explain what they might find inexplicable.

Duccio shows clearly the strange tongues of flame, parted and hovering above each head. The fiery experience leaves all still at peace, lost in prayer, as inwardly, they listen. Jesus called the Holy Spirit a "Paraclete," which means something like "comforter." It is a legal term; the Paraclete is the chief advocate, the supporter of the accused. But Jesus stresses that this Spirit is the Spirit of truth. His comfort is that of showing us the truth and making it possible for us to believe it and obey.

Preparing for the Spirit

Fire burns away dross. The Holy Spirit will purify us. It brings light, and the Holy Spirit will make it impossible for us to ignore reality. And we use fire, for warmth, for cooking, for melting the stiff into the malleable. Any function that helps, we find represented by this bright image, even that it appears as "parted tongues," giving us words when we do not know what to say. It seems crude, speaking like this of so sacred a gift, a gift that is a person. Duccio merely paints in the tongues of fire and concentrates rather on the faces beneath them. All understand that something transforming has happened, and all accept it.

One or two have made what seems like preparations, holding books or scrolls. We can never prepare enough for the Spirit. It is foolish to think that our understanding of the faith ended with our school days. That was the beginning, and it may not even have been a good beginning. (It is extraordinary to hear what impressions some people carry away with them from a Catholic classroom!) It would be a wonderful way to live, peaceful and strong, as Duccio shows us the Twelve, close to Mary, accepting all that the Spirit of Jesus has to give. But these were only ordinary people: they were drawn into this wonder. Why not us too?